Wonders of the World

Niagara Falls

North America's Largest Waterfall

Steve Goldsworthy

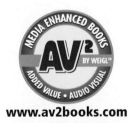

www.av2books.com

AV² provides enriched content that supplements and complements this book. Weigl's AV² books strive to create inspired learning and engage young minds in a total learning experience.

Your AV² Media Enhanced books come alive with...

 Audio
Listen to sections of the book read aloud.

 Key Words
Study vocabulary, and complete a matching word activity.

 Video
Watch informative video clips.

 Quizzes
Test your knowledge.

 Embedded Weblinks
Gain additional information for research.

 Slide Show
View images and captions, and prepare a presentation.

 Try This!
Complete activities and hands-on experiments.

... and much, much more!

Go to **www.av2books.com**, and enter this book's unique code.

BOOK CODE

T 1 2 8 4 1 5

AV² by Weigl brings you media enhanced books that support active learning.

Published by AV² by Weigl
350 5th Avenue, 59th Floor
New York, NY 10118
Websites: www.av2books.com   www.weigl.com

Library of Congress Control Number: 2013953163

ISBN 978-1-4896-0752-2 (hardcover)
ISBN 978-1-4896-0753-9 (softcover)
ISBN 978-1-4896-0754-6 (single user eBook)
ISBN 978-1-4896-0755-3 (multi-user eBook)

Printed in the United States of America in North Mankato, Minnesota
1 2 3 4 5 6 7 8 9 0 18 17 16 15 14

012014
WEP301113

Editor Heather Kissock
Design Mandy Christiansen

Every reasonable effort has been made to trace ownership and to obtain permission to reprint copyright material. The publishers would be pleased to have any errors or omissions brought to their attention so that they may be corrected in subsequent printings.

Photo Credits
Weigl acknowledges Getty Images, Alamy, and Dreamstime as its primary photo supplier for this title.

Contents

A Shared Wonder

Niagara Falls is one of North America's major tourist attractions. Made up of three separate waterfalls, it gushes more than 6 million cubic feet (170,000 cubic meters) of water per minute. It is North America's largest waterfall by **volume**.

Niagara Falls is a wonder shared by two countries. The American Falls and the Bridal Veil Falls are in the State of New York. Horseshoe Falls is in the Canadian province of Ontario. It is the largest and most powerful of the three falls.

Bridal Veil Falls was named after its appearance. It looks like a white bridal veil.

Horseshoe Falls was named for its curved shape. The shape is much like that of a horseshoe.

Niagara Falls Facts

- The word "niagara" is believed to come from the **Iroquois** word *onguiaahra*. This word means "the thunder of waters."
- The Niagara Falls area is known as the Honeymoon Capital of the World. More than 50,000 newlyweds honeymoon at Niagara Falls every year.

- The Horseshoe Falls is more than twice the length of the other two falls. The waterfall on the Canadian side is about 2,200 feet (671 m) long. Together, American and Bridal Veil Falls are only about 1,060 feet (323 m) long.
- At their tallest point, Niagara Falls is about 190 feet (58 m) high.

Map of Niagara Falls

Lake Nipigon

Ontario

Quebec

Lake Superior

C A N A D A

Minnesota

Lake Huron

Lake Michigan

Wisconsin

Lake Ontario

New York

Niagara Falls

LEGEND

Water

● Niagara Falls

⊟ International Border

⊟ State/Provincial Border

Michigan

Lake Erie

Pennsylvania

NJ

N

0   125 Miles

0   125 Kilometers

Indiana   Ohio

U N I T E D   S T A T E S

Many of the 20 million people who visit the falls every year take a boat tour of the site.

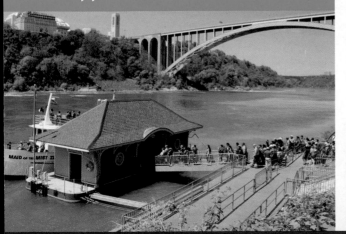

The Skylon Tower provides visitors with an overview of the falls and the surrounding area.

Where in the World?

The waterfall is part of the Great Lakes water system. This vast waterway spans more than 750 miles (1,207 kilometers) from east to west. It includes not only the Great Lakes, but all of the rivers that flow to and from the lakes. One of these rivers is the Niagara River, the river that goes over the falls. The Niagara River is fed by four of the five Great Lakes—Superior, Michigan, Huron, and Erie. After passing Niagara Falls, the river drains into Lake Ontario.

A series of whitewater rapids are located down river from the falls. These waters are known to be the largest rapids navigable by boat.

Both Canada and the United States have paid tribute to Niagara Falls by naming a nearby city after it. Niagara Falls, Ontario, has a population of 83,000 people. Niagara Falls, New York, has about 50,000 people.

Rainbow Bridge straddles the Niagara River Gorge, connecting Niagara Falls, New York, to Niagara Falls, Ontario. Vehicles and pedestrians can use the bridge, which is open 24 hours a day to tourists.

Puzzler

Niagara Falls may be one of the most recognizable waterfalls in the world, but there are many other famous waterfalls. Using an atlas or the internet, match the country to the correct waterfall.

Canada   Iceland   India   New Zealand   United States
Venezuela   Zambia and Zimbabwe

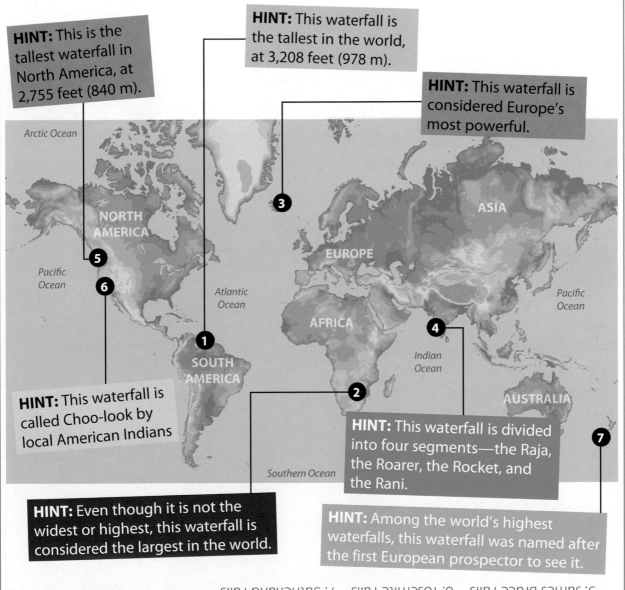

HINT: This is the tallest waterfall in North America, at 2,755 feet (840 m).

HINT: This waterfall is the tallest in the world, at 3,208 feet (978 m).

HINT: This waterfall is considered Europe's most powerful.

HINT: This waterfall is called Choo-look by local American Indians

HINT: This waterfall is divided into four segments—the Raja, the Roarer, the Rocket, and the Rani.

HINT: Even though it is not the widest or highest, this waterfall is considered the largest in the world.

HINT: Among the world's highest waterfalls, this waterfall was named after the first European prospector to see it.

A: 1. Angel Falls   2. Victoria Falls   3. Dettifoss   4. Jog Falls   5. James Bruce Falls   6. Yosemite Falls   7. Sutherland Falls

A Trip Back in Time

The formation of Niagara Falls began at the end of the last Ice Age almost 18,000 years ago. Glaciers began moving southward from what is now Canada's Ontario region. Over centuries, the glaciers carved a **cuesta** into the land, which now serves as the **basin** for most of the Great Lakes. The edge of this cuesta is called the Niagara **Escarpment**. It is a ridge spanning almost 1,000 miles (1,609 km).

As the glaciers melted, they created huge volumes of meltwater. This meltwater filled the cuesta, helping to form the Great Lakes. It also created rivers. One such river was the Niagara River. It formed 12,000 years ago. Land shifted, and glaciers moved across the region over thousands of years. About 5,500 years ago, the Niagara River began pouring over the Niagara Escarpment. Water **eroded** the soft rock below the escarpment. This erosion formed the cliffs of the falls.

The Niagara Escarpment is a horseshoe-shaped ridge that extends through the states of Wisconsin and New York and the Canadian province of Ontario.

How Waterfalls Form

Eventually, all waterfalls will retreat as the overhang collapses and the top of the waterfall erodes. Niagara Falls is retreating at a rate of 1 foot (0.3 m) per year. At this rate, the falls could completely disappear in 50,000 years.

Waterfalls cannot exist without water flow. Water flow begins with **precipitation**. In mountainous areas, snow accumulates during winter. In spring, the snow melts, creating the **runoff** that forms rivers and streams. These streams and rivers then pour into lakes. Lakes overflow, pouring into other rivers. To handle the increased water, the rivers begin cutting channels into the riverbed, causing it to erode.

Riverbeds are made up of different types of rock. Waterfalls usually form in areas where hard rock rests on top of soft rock. Hard rock, such as limestone and dolomite, is resistant to erosion from flowing water. Soft rock, such as crumbly shale, erodes more easily.

As the water flows over the riverbed, the soft rock gradually wears away, leaving a ledge of hard rock. This ledge forms the cliff of the waterfall.

Plants of Niagara Falls

A wide variety of plants thrives in the area surrounding Niagara Falls. The abundance of water in the region helps to create an ideal growing environment. The moderate climate and moist soil allow plants, including flowers, trees, and shrubs, to flourish.

During the end of the last Ice Age, approximately 10,000 years ago, cold-climate plants such as spruce trees and pines trees dominated the area. When **climate change** began to warm the region, plants that enjoyed a warmer climate south of the region began spreading north. The area still hosts its **coniferous** spruce and pine trees, but they now stand beside **deciduous** trees such as oak, elm, maple, and birch.

The Niagara region is known for its fruit-producing trees. Cherry, grape, and plum trees grow along the riverbanks downstream from the falls. Strawberry, raspberry, gooseberry, and blackberry bushes also grow naturally in the region.

Peaches are just one of many fruits grown in the Niagara Region. Approximately 85 per cent of Canadian peaches are produced there.

The Red Mulberry Tree

The red mulberry's berries are a source of food for birds and small animals.

One of the rarest trees native to the Niagara Falls area is the red mulberry. Although it is common in the eastern United States, there are only 21 known trees in the Niagara **gorge**. The red mulberry tree is considered an **endangered species** in the area. The main threat to its survival is its relative, the white mulberry tree. It is cross-breeding with the red mulberry and creating a new type of tree. Scientists suspect the red mulberry is not reproducing enough of its own species because of this.

The Red Mulberry Recovery Team was set up by universities and national parks to study and preserve the tree. The team has developed a number of programs to help preserve the tree and increase its numbers in the region. These programs work to protect the tree's habitat and restrict the growth of the white mulberry.

Wildlife of Niagara Falls

Niagara Falls is part of a diverse and fragile **ecosystem**. A wide variety of animal species share the rich habitat. Mammals such as white-tailed deer, raccoons, foxes, and squirrels live in the woods around the falls. More than 300 species of birds can be sighted in the skies. The waters themselves are home to many kinds of fish.

After years of decline, the bald eagle is making a comeback in the Niagara region. When settlers first arrived in the area, bald eagles were considered common. As people chopped down trees for lumber, the bald eagle's habitat was threatened. People also hunted the eagle to near extinction. It was placed on the endangered list as a result. Today, the bald eagle is a protected animal, and its numbers are rising in the area.

The lake sturgeon is the only native sturgeon found within the Great Lakes and Niagara River. However, over the years, its population has experienced a serious decline. Heavy fishing drove these freshwater fish to near extinction in the early 1900s. Pollution of the Great Lakes has also threatened their survival. The lake sturgeon now has protected status in New York State and Ontario.

Between 1980 and 1985, only two bald eagle nests were found in the entire State of New York. That number has since grown to 124 nests between 2000 and 2005.

A Unique Resident

The northern dusky salamander's lower jaw cannot move. Instead, it opens its mouth by lifting its head.

The northern dusky salamander is one of the rarest animals in the Niagara region. Only one small population exists in the Niagara gorge. These salamanders do not have lungs or gills. Instead, oxygen is absorbed through their mouths and skin.

The Niagara Falls region is ideal for these unique creatures. The gorge's cold, clear streams are rich in oxygen. The waterfall itself provides a damp and misty habitat for these moisture-seeking creatures.

Early Explorers

While the area's American Indians had long been familiar with the waterfall, it was not until 1604 that it became known in other parts of the world. This is when French explorer Samuel de Champlain mentioned it in a report that was sent to Europe. Champlain did not actually see the falls. Instead, he relied on descriptions by the American Indians.

Many believe French explorer Étienne Brûlé was the first European to actually see the falls. In 1615, he was working for Champlain as a scout. His job required him to travel the Great Lakes and the Niagara River extensively. There is, however, no written account of his visit to the waterfall itself.

The first European to write about seeing the falls was a Belgian priest, Father Louis Hennepin. A **missionary** working in the area, he visited Niagara Falls in the winter of 1678. His eyewitness account described the falls as "a waterfall that has no equal."

Samuel de Champlain explored northern New York, the Ottawa River, and the eastern Great Lakes during his many expeditions to the New World.

Pehr Kalm (1716–1779)

Botanist and explorer Pehr (Peter) Kalm was born in Angermanland, Sweden on March 6, 1716. He developed a keen interest in botany while studying at the University of Uppsala in Finland. In 1741, Pehr began studying plants in other parts of the world. After working in Europe for several years, he arrived in the Niagara region in 1750 in search of plant samples to take back to Sweden. Kalm was the first scientist to study the falls, documenting his findings and observations.

Kalm wrote letters to his friend Benjamin Franklin describing his findings. He observed that one part of the waterfall was horseshoe shaped and verified the height of the falls. Benjamin Franklin was so thrilled with Kalm's report that he published it in *The Gentleman's Magazine* as the first scientific account of Niagara Falls.

The Big Picture

Niagara Falls is one of the largest waterfalls in the world by volume. This means that it has more water flowing over it than many of the world's other waterfalls. This map shows some of the other waterfalls known for their volume.

Para Falls
Venezuela
125,000 cu. ft/s (3,540 m³/s)

NORTH AMERICA

PACIFIC OCEAN

ATLANT OCEA

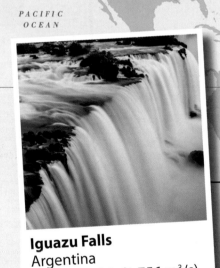

SOUTH AMERICA

Iguazu Falls
Argentina
62,000 cu.ft/s (1,756 m³/s)

Paulo Afonso Falls
Brazil
100,000 cu.ft/s (2,832 m³/s)

LEGEND

☐ Ocean

〜 River

Scale at Equator

0   1,000   2,000   3,000 miles

0   1,000   2,000   3,000 km

N

SOUTHERN OCEAN

ASIA

Khone Falls
Laos
410,000 cu.ft/s (11,610 m³/s)

Niagara Falls
Canada and United States
100,000 cu. ft/s (2,832 m³/s)

EUROPE

PACIFIC
OCEAN

AFRICA

EQUATOR

INDIAN
OCEAN

AUSTRALIA

Victoria Falls
Zambia and Zimbabwe
38,430 cu.ft/s (1,088 m³/s)

SOUTHERN
OCEAN

ANTARCTICA

Living Near Niagara Falls

Scientific evidence indicates that people have lived near Niagara Falls for almost 12,000 years. The earliest group are known as the Clovis people. They were a **nomadic** people who followed the animals that roamed the land. Between 9,000 and 3,000 years ago, hunter-gatherer groups began moving into the area to take advantage of the abundant food sources found along the Niagara River.

Some of the first people to settle in the area were the Iroquois Indians. They began building small villages along the river about 4,000 years ago. Like the hunter-gatherers, they relied on the plants and animals in the area. However, they also began growing their own food. The Iroquois planted crops of beans, squash, and corn in the fertile ground near the Niagara River.

When Europeans arrived in the area, they too began to work the land. Farms and orchards began to appear throughout the area. Sawmills were constructed to take advantage of the forests growing along the river. Over time, **hydroelectric** plants were developed to convert the power of the Niagara River and its falls into electricity for people throughout eastern North America. Today, the falls continue to be a focal point for business and industry in the area.

The Robert Moses Generating Facility in Lewiston, New York, converts the Niagara River's current into power for state residents. The dam was the largest hydroelectric producer in the Western world when it opened in 1961 and is still the main source of electricity for the state of New York.

A National Park

Prospect Point Observation Tower in Niagara Falls State Park offers one of the best panoramic views of the American Falls, Bridal Veil Falls, and Horseshoe Falls.

European settlement in the Niagara Falls region brought many changes to the land. Industries, such as lumber and **textiles**, cropped up along the Niagara River and used its power to operate their factories and mills. As industry grew in the area, many citizens became concerned about the river's health and beauty.

In the 1860s, a group was formed to encourage the New York State government to regain control of the river. Finally, in 1885, the Niagara Appropriations Bill was passed to protect the area. The Niagara Reservation State Park was established at the same time. Situated on the American side of the falls, Niagara Falls State Park covers 400 acres (162 hectares), including the 140 acres (57 ha) covered by the river. It includes American Falls, Bridal Veil Falls, Goat Island, and part of Horseshoe Falls.

Niagara Falls Timeline

Prehistoric

18,000 years ago
Glaciers carve out the Great Lakes.

12,000 years ago
The Niagara River forms and begins flowing over the Niagara Escarpment.

10,000 years ago
The Great Lakes water system begins to drain meltwater, forming many rivers.

9,000 years ago
Hunter-gatherer societies arrive in the region.

4,000 years ago The Iroquois establish villages near Niagara Falls.

Exploration

1604 French explorer Samuel de Champlain writes about the falls in reports that are sent to Europe. His accounts are second-hand, received from local American Indians.

1615 Étienne Brûlé explores the Niagara region for Champlain.

1678 Father Louis Hennepin writes the first eyewitness account of Niagara Falls.

1697 Father Louis Hennepin's book *New Discovery* is published. It features an original sketch of Niagara Falls.

Development

1759 Daniel Joncairs builds the first sawmill in the Niagara region.

1801 Joseph Alston and Theodosia Burr are the first newlyweds to honeymoon at Niagara Falls.

1818 An enclosed staircase is built for visitors to descend to the base of Horseshoe Falls.

1833 Niagara Falls' first luxury hotel, the Clifton Hotel, is built.

May 27, 1846 The ferry *Maid of the Mist* takes its maiden voyage across the Niagara gorge.

1848 The Niagara Suspension Bridge is completed, becoming the first bridge to span the Niagara gorge.

1854 A railroad is built near Niagara Falls, bringing more tourists to the area.

1885 Niagara Falls State Park is established. It is the oldest state park in the United States.

Present

2001 The Flight of Angels balloon ride opens in New York State, offering visitors a birds-eye view of Niagara Falls.

2006 The 175-foot (53-m) tall Niagara Skywheel opens, offering tourists a fantastic view of the falls.

2012 Nik Wallenda is the first person to walk across Horseshoe Falls on a tightrope.

Protecting Niagara Falls

Millions of people visit Niagara Falls every year, making tourism the main industry in the region. However, this many visitors can have a negative impact on the natural area. Both the U.S. and Canadian governments have created programs to ensure that the Niagara Falls natural area is protected from misuse.

Parks are found on both the American and Canadian sides of Niagara Falls. On the United States side is the Niagara Falls State Park. Public spaces and parks on the Canadian side are managed by the Niagara Parks Commission. Park rangers work hard to educate visitors coming to the area. They post signs and give talks to let people know how to behave in the parks. Some of the rules include staying on pathways, disposing of garbage properly, and reporting wildlife sightings. All of these rules help maintain the ecosystems within the park so that erosion is kept to a minimum and plants and animals continue to thrive.

Visitors can learn about the history and preservation of Niagara Falls at the Table Rock Welcome Centre at Niagara Falls in Ontario, Canada. The centre welcomes more than eight million people annually.

Still, with a steady stream of tourists coming to the area every year, maintaining the ecosystem is becoming more difficult. No matter how many rules are in place, there are still people who do not obey them. As well, the area is seeing an increase in business development due to the high tourist traffic. The construction of new buildings, parking lots, and streets takes habitat away from the plants and animals living in the area. This has the potential to force endangered species in the area into extinction.

Should the tourism industry be allowed to develop further in the Niagara Falls region?

Yes	No
Tourism is an import source of income for the local residents of Niagara Falls.	Building hotels and restaurants spoils the natural beauty of the area.
The public receives valuable information on environmental conservation by visiting museums and interpretive centers.	Animal habitats can easily be disturbed by curious tourists.
Tourists can actually help the environment by reporting wildlife sightings or vandalism.	Pollution from powerboats and tour buses harms the natural environment.

The Falls Experience

Niagara Falls attracts visitors from all over the world. To allow these people to experience the falls in person, the site offers several sightseeing opportunities. Some allow people to view the falls at a distance. Others get people all wet.

The observation tower at Prospect Point allows people to view the American Falls from a distance. However, people who want to get closer to the falls can board the *Maid of the Mist*, which docks at the base of the tower. The boats take visitors so close to the falls that raincoats are required clothing.

The Canadian side of the falls offers boat tours as well. Two catamarans travel into the gorge of Horseshoe Falls, giving guests a wet and bumpy ride. To see the falls from the inside, visitors can walk through tunnels that lead to viewing platforms behind the falls. Pathways on both sides of the falls offer breathtaking views of the rushing waters.

In the "Journey Behind the Falls" tour, guests can go behind the Horseshoe Falls by taking an elevator 150 feet (46 m) down through bedrock to a series of underground tunnels. These tunnels lead to two separate viewing platforms.

Daring the Falls

Some visitors prefer to experience Niagara Falls in a more adventurous way. Over the years, Niagara Falls has been the site of many daredevil stunts. People have traveled over the falls in barrels and walked across the gorge below on tightropes. While exciting, these adventures are also very dangerous. People who survive the trip can face fines up to $10,000.

On June 30, 1859, Charles Blondin became the first person to walk across the Niagara gorge on a tightrope.

In July of 1876, Maria Spelterina became the first woman to cross the gorge on tightrope.

Schoolteacher Annie Edson Taylor was the first person to ride over Canada's Horseshoe Falls in a wooden barrel, on October 24th, 1901.

In 2003, Kirk Jones became the first person to go over the falls without equipment and survive. The adventure cost him about $5000 in fines.

The most recent stunt occurred in 2012, when circus performer Nik Wallenda became the first person to cross Horseshoe Falls on a tightrope.

Legends from the Falls

Niagara Falls has fascinated people for a long time. The American Indians who lived in the region saw and heard the waterfall on a constant basis. They felt a connection to it and created stories to explain the important role the waterfall played in their lives.

An Iroquois people called the Seneca tell a story about the Good Spirit of thunder and lightning who lived in the caves behind the falls. The mist he created became clouds in the sky. He also put the thunder in the clouds. Other legends spoke of Great Water Serpents that lived in the river and nearby lakes. These beasts were responsible for poisoning the water and threatening the people. Only by obeying the Good Spirit would the people be spared hardship and death.

The Seneca believed that evil spirits lived at the bottom of the falls. These spirits were responsible for ruining crops and causing other problems.

Maid of the Mist

The boat ride at Niagara Falls takes its name from the legend of the Maid of the Mist.

Another Iroquois group called the Ongiara tell the story of a beautiful young woman who lost her husband. Stricken with grief, she rode a canoe over the falls in an attempt to end her life. Heno, the god of thunder who lived in the falls, caught the young woman and brought her to safety. One of the Heno's sons fell in love with the maiden and married her.

Eventually, a great serpent arrived, threatening the maiden's people. Heno fought with the beast, defeating it. Its body settled in the rapids just before the falls. This made the water rage even more. Heno took his son and the maiden to live in the sky, where Heno continues to make thunder. His mighty powers still echo in the thunder of Niagara Falls.

True or False?

Decide whether the following statements are true or false. If the statement is false, make it true.

1. Niagara Falls is made up of two separate waterfalls.

2. Niagara Falls is shared by both Canada and the United States.

3. The Niagara River began pouring over the Niagara Escarpment about 12,000 years ago.

4. The first European to write an eyewitness account of Niagara Falls was Samuel de Champlain.

5. There is evidence that people have lived near Niagara Falls for almost 12,000 years.

6. The *Maid of the Mist* tour boat operates on the Canadian side of the falls.

ANSWERS

1. False. Niagara Falls is made up of three separate waterfalls. These are American Falls, Bridal Veil Falls, and Horseshoe Falls.
2. True.
3. False. This occurred about 5,500 years ago.
4. False. The first eyewitness account came from Father Louis Hennepin.
5. True.
6. False. It runs on the American side.

Short Answer

Answer the following questions using information from the book.

1. How many people visit Niagara Falls every year?
2. What nickname has Niagara Falls been given?
3. How long is the Niagara Escarpment?
4. When was Niagara Falls State Park established?
5. Who was the first person to walk across Horseshoe Falls on a tightrope?

Multiple Choice

Choose the best answer for the following questions.

1. Which part of Niagara Falls is located in Canada?
   a. Bridal Veil Falls
   b. Horseshoe Falls
   c. American Falls

2. How many Great Lakes feed into the Niagara River?
   a. Three
   b. Four
   c. Five

3. Who provided the first scientific account of Niagara Falls?
   a. Benjamin Franklin
   b. Samuel de Champlain
   c. Pehr Kalm

4. Who are the first people known to live in the Niagara region?
   a. Seneca
   b. Iroquois
   c. Clovis

Activity

Make Your Own Waterfall

A waterfall forms when water flow and varying rock types are combined. Harder rock is resistant to the water's erosion. Softer rock breaks down more quickly. Try this experiment to see how varying layers of rocks can lead to the creation of a waterfall. Please note that this experiment should be attempted outside.

Materials

| A large tub | A large garden slab or piece of wood | A bag of sandbox sand | A bucket of water or a garden hose |

Instructions

1. Fill one side of the large tub with sand. Try to keep the sand on one side only. Fill it level to the top of the tub.

2. Place the slab or piece of wood on top of the sand. Ensure there is sand right up to the edge of the slab underneath.

3. Gently pour water over the slab and into the tub. Notice what happens to the sand directly underneath the slab. Try pouring the water over different spots. Make note of the channels the water erodes in the softer sand.

4. Move the slab back and expose more sand. Repeat steps 1 through 3.

    What would happen if you put fine gravel or pebbles underneath the slab?

Key Words

basin: a large bowl-like land formation

botanist: a scientist who studies plants

climate change: changes in Earth's weather, including temperature, precipitation, and wind patterns

coniferous: a type of tree that bears cones and evergreen needles

cuesta: a ridge with a gentle slope on one side and a steep slope on the other

deciduous: a type of tree that sheds its leaves annually

ecosystem: a biological community of interacting organisms

endangered species: a plant or animal that is at risk of disappearing from Earth

eroded: wore away

escarpment: a steep slope or cliff at the edge of a plateau

gorge: a deep, narrow passage with steep rocky sides

hydroelectric: generating electricity from water such as a rushing river or waterfall

Iroquois: an American Indian group that live throughout New York State and southern Ontario and Quebec

missionary: a person sent on a religious mission

nomadic: moving often, without a fixed settlement

precipitation: any form of moisture falling from the sky, i.e. rain and snow

runoff: the draining away of water

textiles: cloth or woven fabric

volume: an amount or total

Index

Log on to www.av2books.com

AV² by Weigl brings you media enhanced books that support active learning. Go to www.av2books.com, and enter the special code found on page 2 of this book. You will gain access to enriched and enhanced content that supplements and complements this book. Content includes video, audio, weblinks, quizzes, a slide show, and activities.

AV² Online Navigation

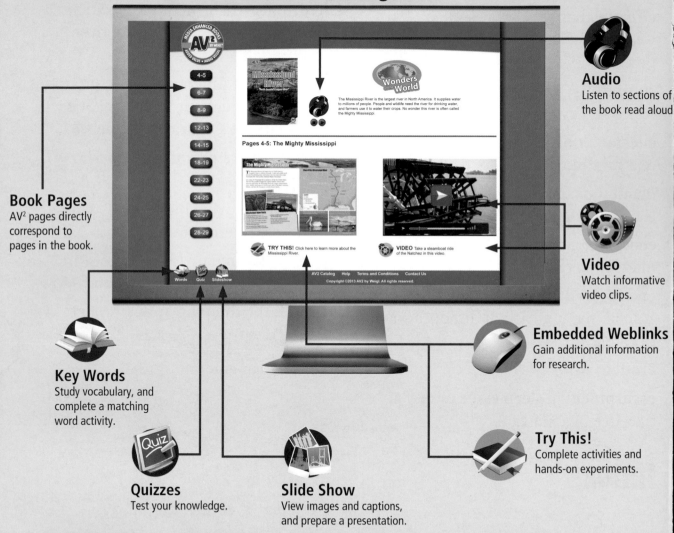

Audio
Listen to sections of the book read aloud

Video
Watch informative video clips.

Embedded Weblinks
Gain additional information for research.

Try This!
Complete activities and hands-on experiments.

Book Pages
AV² pages directly correspond to pages in the book.

Key Words
Study vocabulary, and complete a matching word activity.

Quizzes
Test your knowledge.

Slide Show
View images and captions, and prepare a presentation.

AV² was built to bridge the gap between print and digital. We encourage you to tell us what you like and what you want to see in the future.

Sign up to be an AV² Ambassador at www.av2books.com/ambassador.